THE BOOK EVERY SW... QUESTIONS, QUIZZES, TRIVIA, QUOTES, LIFE LESSONS, STORIES & MORE + BONUS JOURNAL PAGES FOR WRITING YOUR OWN STORY

JESSICA BROWN

Screen Free Fun LLC
2111 S. Magnolia Ave
Tucson, AZ 85711

First Edition, 2024

Library of Congress Cataloging-in-Publication Data is available upon request.

Printed in the United States of America

This Ultimate Taylor Swift Fan Book belongs to:

FOREWORD

Welcome to a journey every Taylor Swift fan dreams of—your own personal all-access pass into the world of Swifties. You're either already a dedicated fan or you're on the cusp of becoming one. Why? Because Taylor Swift is more than just a singer; she's a force of nature in the music world.

Starting from her humble country music beginnings to becoming a pop sensation and beyond, Taylor has captivated hearts worldwide. Her talent for crafting stories through song that resonate on a personal level is unmatched.

"The Ultimate Taylor Swift Fan Book: The Book Every Swiftie Needs – Questions, Quizzes, Trivia, Quotes, Life Lessons, Stories & More + Bonus Journal Pages for Writing Your Own Story" is your gateway into the heart of Taylor's universe. Ever curious about what inspires her unforgettable melodies? Or the key moments that transformed Taylor from an aspiring artist into a global superstar? You're holding the key to those answers and more.

This book is packed with fascinating facts, some you might know and others that will surprise you. It's designed to be a fun exploration of Taylor Swift's world, filled with quizzes to challenge your fan knowledge, journal pages for your own thoughts and stories, and trivia to make you a Swiftie scholar.

Treat this as a shared space with fellow Taylor Swift fans, where you can exchange cherished memories of her music and celebrate the magic that is Taylor. From her very first album to her latest, "Midnights," we'll walk through her musical journey, embracing both the highs and the lows.

So, find a comfy spot, deck out in your Swiftie gear, play your favorite Taylor track, and dive deep into her world. This book celebrates Taylor Swift, her music, and you, her fans, who've passionately supported her through every lyric and melody.

Welcome to the ultimate experience for Taylor Swift fans. The adventure is just beginning!

TABLE OF CONTENTS

Taylor Swift: From Country Roots to Pop Sensation

The Country Beginnings

Once upon a time in Reading, Pennsylvania, a young girl named Taylor Swift picked up a guitar and began to turn tales of love, dreams, and heartbreak into melodies. With her roots firmly planted in country music, Taylor's early songs were a refreshing mix of storytelling and melody, capturing the hearts of listeners with their sincerity and warmth.

Her self-titled debut album, released in 2006, cemented her spot in the country music arena, featuring hits like **"Tim McGraw"** and **"Teardrops on My Guitar"** that touched fans and critics alike. Taylor's ability to connect with her audience through relatable lyrics and captivating performances quickly set her apart in the music industry at a young age.

The Transformation to Pop Stardom

As her music evolved, so did Taylor's ambition. With the release of her album "**Fearless**" in 2008, she began to blur the lines between country and pop, signaling the beginning of a genre-defying career. It was her fourth album, "**Red**," that truly marked Taylor's shift towards a more pop-oriented sound, a move that was both bold and risky. Yet, it paid off spectacularly with the success of "**1989**" in 2014, an album that ditched her acoustic twangs for synth-pop beats and catchy hooks. This album, featuring hits like "**Shake It Off**" and "**Blank Space**," catapulted Taylor into global pop superstardom, earning her critical acclaim and a legion of new fans.

Taylor's journey from country roots to pop sensation is a sheer proof of artistic evolution and fearless experimentation. By embracing change and challenging genre boundaries, Taylor Swift not only reinvented her music but also redefined what it means to be a modern pop artist. Her ability to change and thrive in the ever-changing music industry is a strong proof to her enduring talent and dedication to her craft.

Taylor's Influences: The Artists and Events That Shaped Her Music

Taylor Swift's songs are like a mixtape of her life, blending the different music styles she loves and the big moments she's lived through. Learning about what inspires her music lets us see the heart behind the tunes, showing how her past and what's happening now, her personal stories and what we all go through, come together to make the songs we play over and over and over!

Her Music Heroes

Ever since she was young, Taylor has been inspired by country music greats like **Johnny Cash**, **Dolly Parton**, and the **Dixie Chicks**. They were masters at telling stories with their songs, something that really struck a chord with Taylor and made her want to write music that touches people.

As she grew up, her taste in music expanded to include pop and rock stars like **Shania Twain**, who showed her there's a whole world beyond country music, and **Stevie Nicks** from **Fleetwood Mac**, known for her enchanting performances and deep lyrics.

These artists have left a lasting impression on Taylor and her music—and it shows all throughout her discography!

Life Through Lyrics

Taylor's songs are like pages out of her diary, capturing everything from the thrill of a first crush to the heartache of a breakup. The people she's met, the relationships she's had, and even the rollercoaster of fame—she turns all these experiences into music. This makes her songs feel like they're about our lives, too, letting us see ourselves in her stories. It's this mix of personal tales and sharp observations that has made her music a hit with fans, creating a connection that goes beyond just the notes.

The Fame Factor

Becoming a worldwide star has also shaped Taylor's music. Dealing with all the attention and the pressure has inspired her to write about finding out who you really are, managing your reputation, and staying true to yourself in a world that's always watching. These reflections add another layer to her music, making it resonate with anyone who appreciates the realness and raw emotion she brings to her songs.

Swiftie Expertise

Test your knowledge!

1. What was Taylor Swift's debut single?
A) "Love Story"
B) "Tim McGraw"
C) "Teardrops on My Guitar"
D) "Our Song"

2. Taylor Swift has a famous track that was extended into a 10-minute version—what song is it?
A) "Style"
B) "Dear John"
C) "Joe"
D) "All Too Well"

3. Which album did Taylor Swift re-record first?
A) "1989"
B) "Fearless"
C) "Speak Now"
D) "Red"

4. What is the name of Taylor Swift's documentary on Netflix?
A) "Miss Americana"
B) "The Swift Life"
C) "Journey to Fearless"
D) "Taylor Swift: Reputation Stadium Tour"

5. Taylor Swift moved to Nashville at a young age to pursue music. How old was she?
A) 12
B) 13
C) 14
D) 15

Swiftie Expertise

Test your knowledge!

6. Which song did Taylor Swift write in response to media scrutiny and dating rumors?
A) "Mean"
B) "Shake It Off"
C) "Blank Space"
D) "The Man"

7. What is Taylor Swift's lucky number?
A) 7
B) 13
C) 22
D) 1989

8. For which song did Taylor Swift win her first Grammy?
A) "You Belong With Me"
B) "White Horse"
C) "Bad Blood"
D) "Shake It Off"

9. Taylor Swift made her acting debut in which movie?
A) "Valentine's Day"
B) "The Giver"
C) "Cats"
D) "Miss Americana"

10. How many cats does Taylor Swift have, and what are their names?
A) One: Meredith
B) Two: Meredith and Olivia
C) Three: Meredith, Olivia, and Benjamin
D) Four: Meredith, Olivia, Benjamin, and Diana

1.B 2.D 3.B 4.A 5.C 6.C 7.B 8.B 9.A 10.C

Taylor Swift

The Start of a Journey

In **2006**, a young singer-songwriter from Pennsylvania released her debut album, simply titled **"Taylor Swift,"** marking the beginning of what would become a monumental career in music. This album introduced the world to Taylor Swift's heartfelt storytelling and country twang, cementing her talent in turning personal experiences into relatable songs.

"Taylor Swift" was a breath of fresh air in the country music scene, with Taylor writing or co-writing every song on the album—a rarity for a debut artist. The lead single, **"Tim McGraw,"** was a great starter proof of her country influences and set the tone for the album's style. Other hits like **"Teardrops on My Guitar"** and **"Our Song"** further established Taylor as a gifted storyteller, capable of capturing the highs and lows of teenage life with honesty and charm.

The album was more than just a collection of songs; it was a glimpse into Taylor's world, her dreams, and her heartaches. It resonated with listeners of all ages, earning Taylor a dedicated fanbase and laying the groundwork for her journey from country sweetheart to global superstar.

Fan Favorites (5)

- Teardrops on My Guitar
- Our Song
- Tim McGraw
- Should've Said No
- Mary's Song (Oh My My My)

Fearless

A Powerful Sophomore Album

In **2008**, Taylor Swift took a bold step forward with her sophomore album, "Fearless." This album not only solidified her status as a country music star but also hinted at her crossover appeal, mixing country with hints of pop. "Fearless" was a tour de force, showcasing Taylor's growth as a songwriter and her ambition to reach beyond the boundaries of country music.

The album featured hits like **"Love Story"** and **"You Belong With Me,"** songs that transcended country music to become global anthems. "Love Story," with its timeless tale of Romeo and Juliet set against a catchy melody, and "You Belong With Me," a classic high school anthem of liking someone who already has a partner, captured the hearts of listeners worldwide. These tracks helped **"Fearless"** become the best-selling album of 2009 in the United States.

That said, "Fearless" was more than just an album; it was a statement of Taylor's artistic vision and her ability to connect with fans on a personal level. It even won four **Grammy Awards**, including **Album of the Year**, making Taylor the youngest artist ever to win this prestigious award at the time!

Fan Favorites (5)

- Love Story
- Hey Stephen
- You Belong With Me
- White Horse
- The Way I Loved You

Speak Now

A Storytelling Force

In **2010**, Taylor Swift boldly carved a new path in her career with the launch of **"Speak Now,"** an album where every song sprang from her own pen. This was a significant milestone, as it proved Taylor's independence as an artist and reflected her growth both personally and professionally.

This album lets us go through richer emotional scenes, capturing everything from the romance in **"Mine"** to the introspective **"Dear John,"** revealing Taylor's evolving skill in turning personal tales into songs with catchy beats and hooks. The song **"Mean"** particularly stands out, confronting themes of bullying and resilience, and struck a chord with listeners for its message of empowerment.

It's no surprise that **"Speak Now"** was a smash hit, rocketing to the top of the Billboard 200 chart and reinforcing Taylor's powerhouse status in the music industry. It was definitely a strong proof of her versatility as an artist—fearless in writing about different situations all while retaining her distinctive storytelling style people worldwide have come to love!

Fan Favorites (5)

- Mine
- Back to December
- Dear John
- Better Than Revenge
- I Can See You

Red

The Transition

2012's "Red" was a game-changer for Taylor Swift, marking the proper start of her transition from a country sensation to a pop icon. This album saw Taylor diving headfirst into a mix of musical styles, from the catchy tunes of **"We Are Never Ever Getting Back Together"** to the deep, heartfelt **"All Too Well." "Red"** became Taylor's lab for mixing rock, electronic sounds, and timeless pop with her country style.

The lyrics on "Red" show the ups and downs of relationships and feelings, earning praise for its emotional depth and maturity. The album was a hit factory, cementing Taylor's spot in the pop scene while paying respect to her country origins. Tracks like **"I Knew You Were Trouble"** and the main song **"Red"** showed Taylor's skill in covering the full range of pop music, proof of her wide-ranging appeal.

But **"Red"** did more than just expand Taylor Swift's range of music; it also brought her a wider audience, pulling in fans from all over the world and with different music tastes. It locked in her position as an international star who could cross over music styles and break barriers.

Fan Favorites (5)

- All Too Well
- State of Grace
- Holy Ground
- Nothing New (feat. Phoebe Bridgers)
- The Very First Night

1989
The Pop Breakthrough

In **2014**, Taylor Swift came out with **"1989,"** an album that didn't just mark her full shift to pop music but also gave the genre a fresh new look. Named after the year she was born, **"1989"** showed off a Taylor Swift who was ready to leave behind any old labels and start anew with bold confidence. This album was her big move away from country music, embracing the upbeat and catchy world of synth-pop in a way that surprised and captivated listeners everywhere.

"1989" featured a mix of songs that paid tribute to the 1980s pop tunes Taylor loved as a kid while also pushing the boundaries of what pop music could be. Hits like **"Shake It Off"** and **"Blank Space"** showed Taylor's knack for making catchy, memorable songs that bit back to her critics and anyone who only saw her as a serial dater. These songs, along with others like **"Style"** and **"Bad Blood,"** mixed clever lyrics with tunes you couldn't get out of your head—easily making **"1989"** a standout pop album.

But **"1989"** wasn't just a hit in terms of sales; critics loved it too. It won Taylor Swift her second **Grammy for Album of the Year**, making her the first woman to win this top award twice. Critics applauded **"1989"** for how well it stuck together as a whole and for tackling big topics like fame, who you are, and the ups and downs of relationships, all with a polished sound that still felt genuine and heartfelt.

The Impact of *1989*

"1989" was more than just a key album for Taylor Swift; it was also something that shaped the future of pop music. Taylor's move to include synth-pop and electronic beats opened the door to a fresh style of pop music that felt both old and new at the same time.

The music videos for **"1989"** also made a huge impact at the peak of its fame. From the fun, self-mocking **"Shake It Off"** to the satire depiction of her in **"Blank Space,"** these videos trickled their way to the mainstream media—a salt on the wound for haters who thought she's just a good-for-nothing heartbreaker in the industry!

With **"1989,"** Taylor Swift also started a new chapter in how she connects with her fans. She got creative with social media and marketing, making fans feel closer to her by inviting them to special album listening parties and showing them what goes on behind the scenes. This didn't just make her bond with her fans stronger; it also changed the game for how artists and fans interact online.

It's an understatement to say that releasing **"1989"** was a *huge* moment in Taylor Swift's career—as it confirmed her as one of the biggest names in pop music. The album's success truly showed how flexible Taylor is as an artist and how she can magnificently turn the tables around and make a song out of the narratives thrown against her. "1989" isn't just a peak moment in Taylor Swift's career; it's a game-changer for pop music, proving that, indeed, she is the music industry!

Fan Favorites (5)

- Style
- Is It Over Now?
- Clean
- Out of the Woods
- You Are In Love

Reputation

A Bold New Direction

In **2017**, Taylor Swift took a dramatic turn with the release of **"Reputation,"** an album that put into focus the media's perception of her, the value of privacy in her life, and the complexities of love in the spotlight. This album marked a significant departure from the bright pop of **"1989,"** embracing a darker, more edgy aesthetic. With heavy beats, sharp synths, and a defiant tone, "Reputation" showcased Taylor Swift in a new light—as an artist unafraid to confront her critics and take control of her narrative.

"Reputation" was a musical exploration of Taylor's struggles and triumphs, featuring hits like **"Look What You Made Me Do,"** which served as a bold rebuttal to public scrutiny, and **"Delicate,"** a vulnerable song about love when you are always under the intense gaze of the public eye. The album's sound was a mix of intense pop and electro, with elements of hip-hop, proving Taylor's versatility and willingness to experiment with even newer styles.

Despite its shift in tone, **"Reputation"** was a commercial powerhouse, debuting at No. 1 on the Billboard 200 chart and becoming the best-selling album of 2017 in the U.S. It reaffirmed Taylor's mastery of the pop genre in a completely different page!

Fan Favorites (5)

- Delicate
- Gorgeous
- Getaway Car
- Don't Blame Me
- Call It What You Want

Lover

A Return to Light

Following the introspective darkness and edgy aesthetics of **"Reputation,"** Taylor Swift's **2019** album **"Lover"** felt like a breath of fresh air. With its vibrant pastel hues and romantic themes, **"Lover"** was a celebration of love in all its forms. This album marked a return to the more upbeat, synth-pop sound that fans had fallen in love with, while also exploring new territory with elements of dream pop, indie, and even some country-flavored tracks.

"Lover" stood out for its sincere and deep lyrics, ranging from the romantic lyricism of songs like **"Daylight"** and **"Cornelia Street"** to the bold **"You Need to Calm Down,"** which supported LGBTQ+ rights. Tracks like "**Miss Americana & The Heartbreak Prince"** blended pop tunes with serious comments on society, showing Taylor's ability to create catchy songs that also make you think.

Commercially and critically acclaimed, **"Lover"** was a testament to Taylor Swift's enduring appeal and her ability to continuously evolve as an artist. It debuted at No. 1 on the Billboard 200 chart and was praised for its eclectic sound and emotional depth—which is already a staple for any work of Taylor's!

Fan Favorites (5)

- Cruel Summer
- Lover
- Miss Americana & The Heartbreak Prince
- Cornelia Street
- Daylight

folklore

A Surprise Turn to Indie Folk

In **2020**, Taylor Swift shocked fans and the music world by dropping "folklore," an album that veered into indie folk, a style far removed from her previous pop hits. With its quiet, introspective tunes and story-driven songs, "folklore" felt like a cozy blanket, wrapping listeners in its moody, reflective vibe.

"folklore" features songs like "invisible string," which quickly became a favorite by hopeless romantics, and "the 1," known for its bittersweet reflection on what could have been. Taylor collaborated with indie artists like Bon Iver on "exile," blending their voices in a powerful duet that stands out as a highlight of the album. This album also featured a fictional love triangle in the form of three songs: "betty," "cardigan," and "august."

The music in "folklore" combines gentle guitar strums, soft piano melodies, and Taylor's clear voice to create a sound that's both new and timeless—a thing that invited a lot of new fans into the Swiftie wormhole!

Fan Favorites (5)

- this is me trying
- the 1
- mirrorball
- august
- invisible string

evermore

The Other Half "folklore"

Riding the wave of **"folklore's"** success, Taylor Swift released **"evermore"** later in 2020, surprising fans once again. This album continued the indie folk journey, exploring even more emotional stories. If **"folklore"** was a step into a new world, then **"evermore"** was a deeper exploration of that terrain, offering a mix of melancholy, hope, and everything in between.

With tracks like **"willow,"** which explores the twists and turns of fate and love, and "no body, no crime," a storytelling song with a twist of mystery, "evermore" solidifies Taylor's skill in crafting songs that feel like chapters in a book. The collaboration with HAIM on **"no body, no crime"** and another team-up with Bon Iver for "evermore" show Taylor's seamless ability to merge her style with others and creating a song that does not disappoint.

"evermore" received heaps of praise for its lyrical depth and musical beauty—with fans dubbing it as the elder sister of "folklore." Together, the two albums represent a significant period in Taylor Swift's career, a clear proof of how she is still capable of outdoing herself in the department of songwriting.

Fan Favorites (5)

- tolerate it
- long story short
- gold rush
- champagne problems
- willow

Midnights

Opening a New Chapter

In a move that excited fans worldwide, Taylor Swift released **"Midnights"** in 2022, an album that marked yet another bold step in her ever-evolving musical journey.

"Midnights" is described by Taylor as a collection of songs written in the middle of the night, a time when thoughts run wild and emotions are at their peak. This album dives into personal stories, reflections, and the kinds of thoughts that keep you awake at night, offering listeners a window into Taylor's world like never before.

With **"Midnights,"** Taylor mixes pop sounds with electronic and synth elements, creating a sound that is both modern and reminiscent of her previous work. Songs like **"Anti-Hero"** and **"Lavender Haze"** quickly rose to fame for their catchy melodies and relatable lyrics, touching on themes of self-reflection, love, and the challenges of fame.

Like all her previous works, Taylor's storytelling shines brightly in this album, with each track serving as a deeply personal confession or story, making the album resonate with anyone who's ever found themselves lost in thought at midnight.

What "**Midnights**" Brings to the Table

"Midnights" wasn't just another album from Taylor Swift; it became a major event in 2022, showing how much of an impact Taylor has on music and pop culture. The album, with its deep look into personal and late-night thoughts, really reached people, getting a lot of praise for how it digs deep emotionally and brings something new to the music.

Taylor's work on **"Midnights"** shows her knack for making an album that's more than just music. Each song, with its stories and sounds, draws you into a night filled with deep thoughts and discoveries. The album connects with the common feeling of lying awake at night, wrestling with your thoughts, making it a strong friend for those long, sleepless nights.

"Midnights" stands out as proof of Taylor Swift's ongoing ability to surprise and move her audience. This album isn't just music; it's a journey through the ups and downs of life, set to the quiet of nighttime.

Fan Favorites (5)

- You're On Your Own, Kid
- Bejeweled
- Midnight Rain
- Mastermind
- Karma

Design Your Own **Album Cover Art**

What would you come up with if given the chance to revamp and design Taylor Swift's album cover designs from scratch? Let's see!

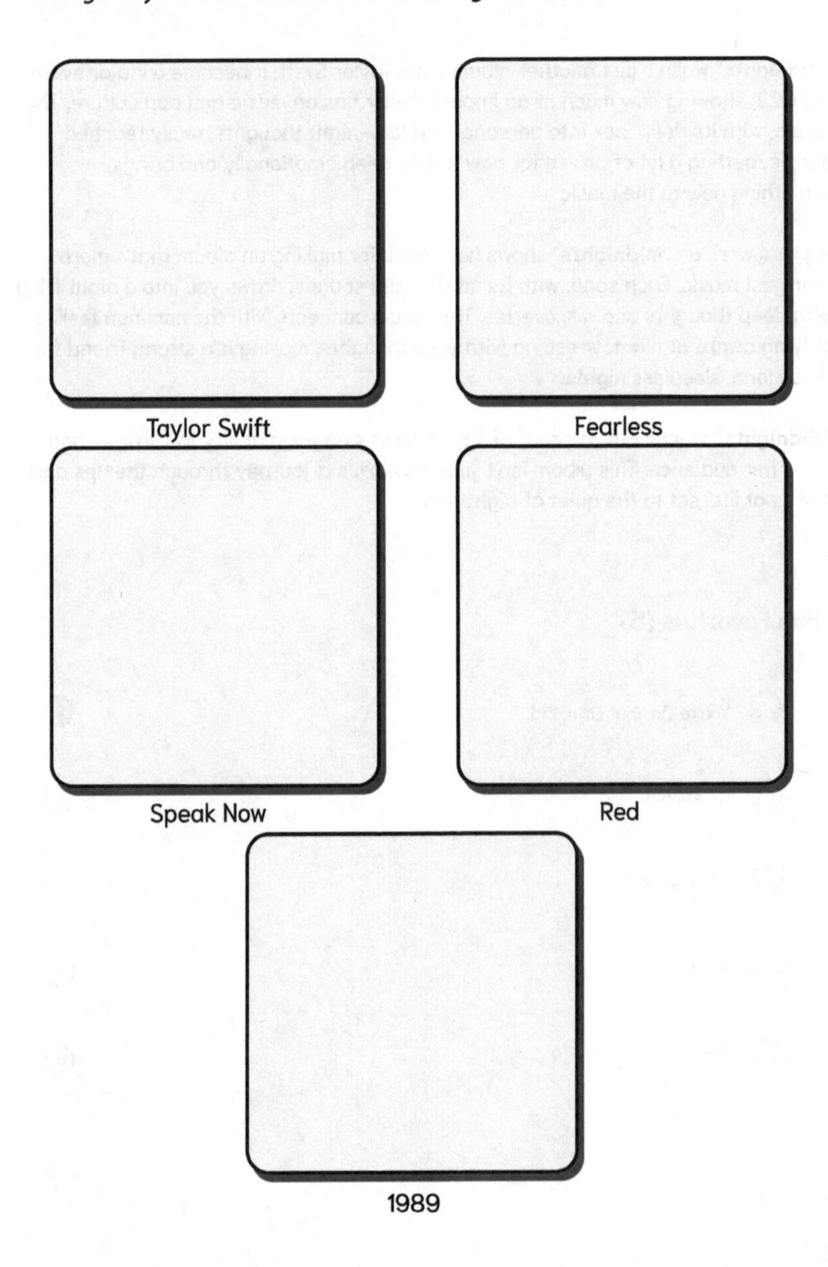

Taylor Swift

Fearless

Speak Now

Red

1989

Design Your Own
Album Cover Art

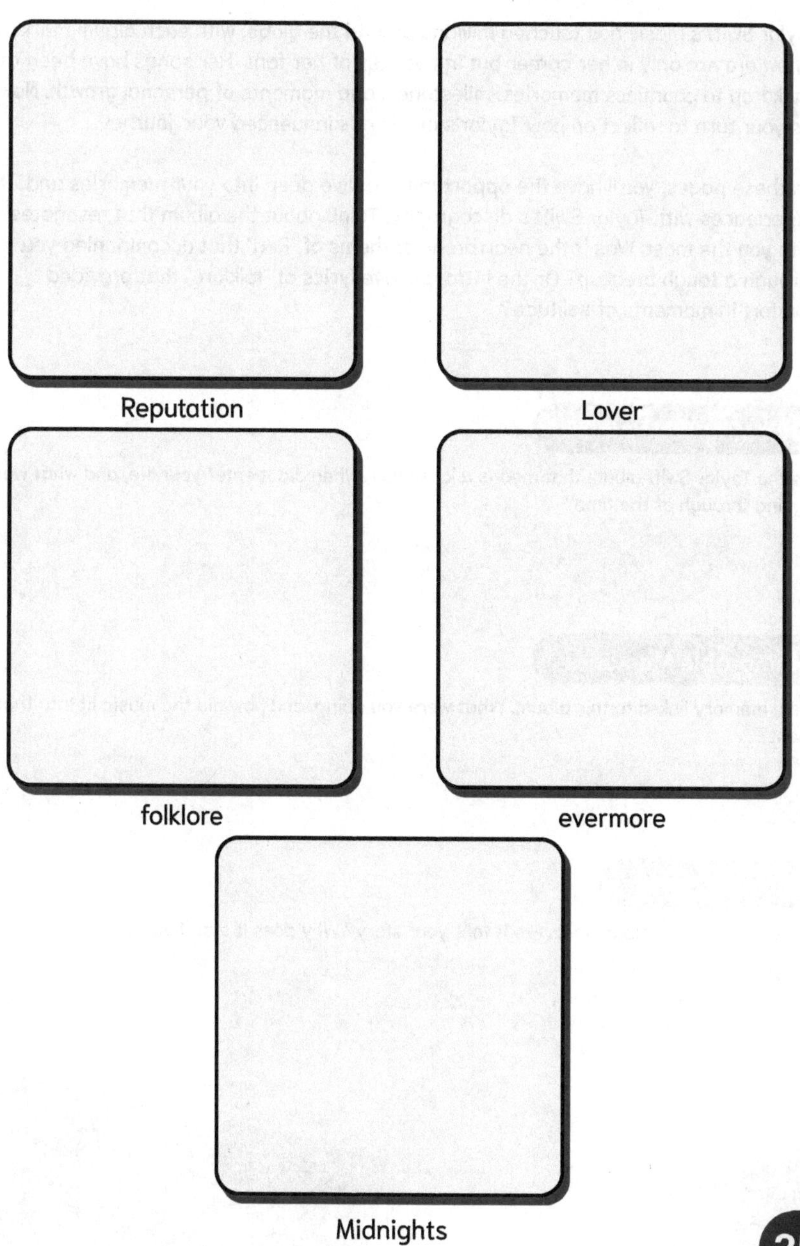

The Taylor Swift Album That Changed My Life

Taylor Swift's music has touched millions around the globe, with each album marking a new era not only in her career but in the lives of her fans. Her songs have been the backdrop to countless memories, milestones, and moments of personal growth. Now, it's your turn to reflect on how Taylor's music has influenced your journey.

On these pages, you'll have the opportunity to dive deep into your memories and experiences with Taylor Swift's discography. Think about the album that resonates with you the most. Was it the heartbreak anthems of "Red" that accompanied you through a tough breakup? Or the introspective lyrics of "folklore" that provided comfort in moments of solitude?

Choosing Your Album

Name the Taylor Swift album that means a lot to you. When did it enter your life, and what were you going through at the time?

Memorable Moments

Share a memory linked to this album. What were you doing, and how did the music fit into that moment?

Favorite Song

Which song from the album feels like it tells your story? Why does it stand out to you?

Lyrics That Resonate

Is there a line from the album that feels like it was written for you? How has it impacted you?

Life Lessons

How has this album shaped your views on love, loss, or personal growth?

A Note to Taylor

If you could tell Taylor Swift about the impact of this album on your life, what would you say?

The Album's Impact

How has this album influenced who you are today, and how will it continue to be part of your story?

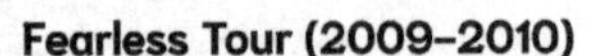

Mapping Taylor Swift's Tours

Over the years, Taylor Swift has taken her music around the world, captivating millions of fans with her exciting live performances. From intimate country music halls to packed stadiums in major cities, her global tours have not only expanded her fan base but have also marked significant milestones in her career.

Fearless Tour (2009–2010)
Taylor's first major tour, mixing her country roots with emerging pop vibes and introducing her to the global stage.

Speak Now World Tour (2011–2012)
A theatrical showcase of Taylor's evolving storytelling, featuring elaborate sets and costumes.

The Red Tour (2013–2014)
A step up in sophistication and energy, this tour drew larger audiences and showcased Taylor's pop power.

The 1989 World Tour (2015)
Celebrating her pop transformation, this tour was known for its high production and guest stars, affirming Taylor's status as a pop icon.

Reputation Stadium Tour (2018)
Taylor's biggest tour back then, combining high-energy performances with stunning visuals, setting new records.

Lover Fest (Planned for 2020, Canceled): Intended as a festival-style
A celebration of the "Lover" album, it was canceled due to the pandemic.

Make Your Own Tour Setlist

Put yourself in the shoes of the mastermind behind Taylor Swift's next worldwide tour. Your mission is to build the ultimate setlist, touching on every chapter of Taylor's music career, from her country start to her indie folk stories and pop hits.

Here's your chance to pick the Taylor Swift songs that mean the most to you and fit perfectly into the concert of your dreams. Think about how the show should flow, the feelings you want to bring out, and how to mix well-known hits with hidden treasures for the true fans!

Opening Act

Pick the opening song. What vibe do you want to set?

Country Roots

Choose 2-3 country songs that show where Taylor started.

Pop Hits

Select 3-4 pop songs that everyone knows and loves.

Indie Folk Moments

Pick 2 indie folk songs from "Folklore" and "Evermore."

Hidden Gems

Choose 2-3 lesser-known songs that hold a special place.

Grand Finale

Decide on the closing song that leaves everyone wallowing in their emotions!

The Glory of *The Eras Tour*

"The Eras Tour" is the biggest concert series from Taylor Swift, envisioned as a grand celebration of her musical journey—all for the right reasons. This tour, which runs for three hours, is designed as a living timeline, taking fans on a trip through the different phases of Taylor's career. From her country beginnings to her pop dominance and indie folk explorations, **"The Eras Tour"** is a showcase of Taylor's versatility as an artist and her evolution over the years.

Each segment is a carefully curated experience, with setlists that cover the entire spectrum of Taylor's discography. Fans get to hear their favorite hits from each era, along with deep cuts and fan favorites, all performed with the energy and passion Taylor is known for!

BONUS

Want More Facts That You Won't Find Anywhere Else?

Unlock 31 Taylor Swift facts that you can't find online!

Plus, you'll get a free 55-page bonus Taylor Swift activity book full of tons of extra activities.

Scan the QR code or use the link below to get your bonuses now!

www.swiftiesuperfans.com/ultimate-freebies

The Eras Tour
Setlist

Lover Era
- 'Miss Americana and The Heartbreak Prince'
- 'Cruel Summer'
- 'The Man'
- 'You Need to Calm Down'
- 'Lover'
- 'The Archer'

Fearless Era
- 'Fearless'
- 'You Belong With Me'
- 'Love Story'

Evermore Era
- ''Tis the damn season'
- 'Willow'
- 'Marjorie'
- 'Champagne Problems'
- 'Tolerate It'

Reputation Era
- '...Ready for It?'
- 'Delicate'
- 'Don't Blame Me'
- 'Look What You Made Me Do'

The Speak Now Era
- 'Enchanted'
- 'Long Live'

The Red Era
- '22'
- 'We Are Never Ever Getting Back Together'
- 'I Knew You Were Trouble'
- 'All Too Well (10 Minute Version)'

The Folklore Era
- 'The 1'
- 'Betty'
- 'The Last Great American Dynasty'
- 'August'
- 'Illicit Affairs'
- 'My Tears Ricochet'
- 'Cardigan'

The 1989 Era
- 'Style'
- 'Blank Space'
- 'Shake It Off'
- 'Wildest Dreams'
- 'Bad Blood'

The Midnights Era
- 'Lavender Haze'
- 'Anti-Hero'
- 'Midnight Rain'
- 'Vigilante Shit'
- 'Bejeweled'
- 'Mastermind'
- 'Karma'

The Eras Tour

Breaking Records Worldwide

In 2023, Taylor Swift took the world by storm with **"The Eras Tour,"** her biggest series of concerts yet. This tour was a massive celebration of Taylor's music, covering her entire career with 152 shows across five continents. It wasn't just a concert series; it became a record-breaking event that showed Taylor's huge impact on music and beyond.

Record-Breaking Tour

"The Eras Tour" *did something incredible in just eight months: it earned over $1 billion, making it the highest-grossing tour ever. With over 4.3 million tickets sold for just the shows in 2023, Taylor beat records set by music legends like Elton John. And with more shows to come, experts think she might even reach $2 billion in earnings.*

Packed Stadiums

Taylor shattered attendance records at famous venues around the world. From Nashville to Melbourne, she drew the largest crowds ever, even creating a new kind of record for having thousands of fans celebrating outside the venues in ***"Taygating"*** *parties.*

Boosting Craft Sales

Taylor's influence reached even the craft world. A single lyric from her ***"Midnights"*** *album (listen to* ***"You're On Your Own, Kid"****) sparked a friendship bracelet craze, skyrocketing sales in craft stores and inspiring fans and even other fandoms to embrace this trend.*

A Groundbreaking Concert Film

*Taylor's decision to release **"The Eras Tour"** concert film changed the game, earning $250 million at the box office and becoming the highest-grossing concert film of all time. It even got a Golden Globe nomination, competing with major movies.*

Economic Impact

***"The Eras Tour"** didn't just entertain; it boosted local economies. Fans spent an average of $1,300 per person at each tour stop, similar to the economic impact of hosting 53 Super Bowls across the country.*

Social Media Sensation

*Online, **"The Eras Tour"** was everywhere. TikTok live streams of the concerts attracted tens of thousands of viewers, and Taylor-related content saw millions of views daily.*

Chart-Topping Music

*The tour also sent Taylor's music soaring up the charts. Songs performed on tour saw huge increases in streaming, with **"Cruel Summer"** becoming a number one hit years after its release.*

Concert Checklist ✓

Get Ready for the Show of a Lifetime

Going to a Taylor Swift concert is an unforgettable experience. Whether you're a first-timer or a seasoned concert-goer, being prepared can make the day even more magical. Here's your ultimate checklist to ensure you're ready for the show of a lifetime.

Must-Haves

- ☐ **Ticket:** Keep it on your phone or have a printed copy.
- ☐ **ID & Money:** For merch and ID checks.
- ☐ **Power Bank:** Don't miss capturing special moments!

Wear & Care

- ☐ **Outfit & Shoes:** Dress up in your Swiftie best but keep it comfy.
- ☐ **Weather Gear:** Check the weather—bring a raincoat or sunscreen if needed.

Fan Fun

- ☐ **Lights & Signs:** Brighten up the night and show your support.
- ☐ **Fan Project Items:** If you're joining a fan action, remember your part!

Stay Healthy

- ☐ **Water & Snacks:** Stay hydrated and energized.
- ☐ **Earplugs:** Enjoy the music safely.

Stay Connected

- ☐ **Plan with Friends:** Know where to meet before and after the show.

Extras

- ☐ **Merch Budget:** Save some cash for tour merch.
- ☐ **Camera/Phone:** Ready for photos and videos.

Before You Go

- ☐ **Venue Rules:** Check what you can bring.
- ☐ **Transport Plan:** Know how you're getting there and back.

Taylor Swift:

The Stories Behind the Lyrics

It's well-established that Taylor Swift is not just a singer; she's a storyteller. Her songs are windows into her life, filled with personal stories, vivid imagery, and emotions that resonate with fans worldwide. From tales of love and heartbreak to reflections on fame and self-discovery, Taylor's lyrics invite listeners into her world. Let's explore the stories behind some of her most iconic songs:

"All Too Well"

Often hailed as one of her best songs, "All Too Well" recounts the details of a past relationship and its painful aftermath. Known for its emotional depth and vivid storytelling, the song strikes a chord with anyone who's experienced a difficult breakup. The scarf mentioned in the song has become a symbol of lost love among fans.

"Shake It Off"

With "Shake It Off," Taylor addresses the criticism and rumors that come with fame. It's a fun, upbeat anthem about ignoring the haters and being true to yourself.

"The Man"

In "The Man," Taylor explores the double standards faced by women in the music industry and beyond. The song imagines how her career might have differed had she been male, showing the challenges women face in achieving recognition and respect.

"Cardigan"

Part of the "folklore" album, "cardigan" tells the story of a teenage love triangle from different perspectives.

"Betty"

"Betty" continues the love triangle story from "Cardigan," but from the perspective of the boy who made a mistake.

How Taylor Writes Her Lyrics in Different Pens

During an acceptance speech at the Nashville Songwriter Awards, where she was honored as the Songwriter-Artist of the Decade, Taylor Swift gave us a peek into her creative mind. She imagines writing her songs with three different types of pens: **Quill Pen, Fountain Pen**, and **Glitter Gel Pen**, each symbolizing a distinct style of her songwriting process.

Fountain Pen Songs

These are the songs that feel like modern poetry, sharing personal stories that resonate deeply. They're the tunes that stick with you, painting vivid pictures of emotions and experiences. **"False God"** and **"Cruel Summer"** from **"Lover"**, along with **"exile"** featuring Bon Iver from **"folklore",** are prime examples. They're introspective and rich, reflecting on moments that linger in the mind.

Listen to

PLAY

SONG TITLE	ALBUM
♥ The Archer	Lover
♥ Cornelia Street	Lover
♥ White Horse	Fearless - Taylor's Version
♥ Cruel Summer	Lover
♥ Treacherous	Red - Taylor's Version
♥ long story short	evermore
♥ All Too Well (10 Minute version)	Red - Taylor's Version
♥ State of Grace	Red - Taylor's Version
♥ I Almost Do	Red - Taylor's Version
♥ Holy Ground	Red - Taylor's Version
♥ Lover	Lover

Quill Pen Songs

Quill Pen songs transport you to another era, echoing the style of old-world poets writing by the flicker of candlelight. This category includes songs like **"ivy"** from **"evermore"** and **"my tears ricochet"** from **"folklore"**. These tracks weave tales that feel both historic and deeply emotional, crafting narratives that seem timeless.

Listen to PLAY

SONG TITLE	ALBUM
ivy	evermore
happiness	evermore
Carolina	Where the Crawdad's Sing soundtrack
evermore feat. Bon Iver	evermore
cowboy like me	evermore
hoax	folklore
epiphany	folklore
the last great american dynasty	folklore
peace	folklore

Glitter Gel Pen Songs

Then, there are the Glitter Gel Pen tracks – the ones that burst with energy and fun. These are the songs that make you want to dance and belt out the lyrics without a care. Hits like **"We Are Never Ever Getting Back Together"** from **"Red (Taylor's Version)"** and **"You Need to Calm Down"** from **"Lover"** belong here. They serve as lighthearted reminders to enjoy life and not sweat the small stuff.

Listen to PLAY

SONG TITLE	ALBUM
I Forgot That You Existed	Lover
22	Red – Taylor's Version
You Belong With Me	Fearless – Taylor's Version
I Think He Knows	Lover
London Boy	Lover
You Need to Calm Down	Lover
Hey Stephen	Fearless – Taylor's Version

The Fictional Characters in Taylorverse

In 2020, Taylor Swift surprised everyone not once, but three times. First, she dropped the album 'folklore' out of the blue, then she released its follow-up 'evermore', and also introduced us to a fresh way of writing songs. This time, her music wasn't just about her own experiences but also included stories about made-up characters and people from her past who are no longer with us. Let's dive into the world of 'folklore' and get to know these characters:

Rebekah Harkness

In the song "the last great american dynasty," Taylor Swift tells us about **Rebekah Harkness**, linking a true story with Taylor's own life. Rebekah, who once lived in the same house Taylor bought, faced a lot of talk and judgment because of her fame, much like Taylor herself. Through Rebekah's life, Taylor explores how tough it can be to stay true to yourself when everyone has an opinion on who you should be.

Dean

"epiphany" is a tribute to Taylor's granddad, **Dean**, a hero of World War II. Taylor draws a touching link between his brave but silent fight and the battle against COVID-19, showing us the strength in quiet bravery and the heroes who don't always get celebrated.

Marjorie Finlay

"marjorie" is a heartfelt song where Taylor Swift remembers her grandmother, **Marjorie Finlay**, an opera singer. This song beautifully mixes feelings of loss with appreciation for the lessons and love our lost ones leave behind. Through "marjorie," Taylor shares how her grandmother's legacy and advice continue to influence her, reminding us to hold on to the precious memories and wisdom of those we've lost.

James

Then, there's **James**, a character in a story of young love gone wrong. In "betty," James is a teenager who messes up and tries to say sorry to his girlfriend, Betty. James' story, inspired by the name of Ryan Reynolds and Blake Lively's daughter, touches on the mistakes we make in love and the hope for forgiveness.

Betty

Betty, on the other hand, shares her feelings in "cardigan," thinking back on James' mistake with both understanding and hurt. Also named after one of Reynolds and Lively's daughters, Betty shows us the pain and beauty of first love, mixing wisdom with the innocence of youth.

Augustine

"August" introduces us to **Augustine**, the "other woman" in James' summer fling. Augustine's story is a sad look at a short-lived romance, reminding us of the ones who end up alone when summer love fades away.

Inez

Lastly, **Inez** is the one who spills the beans about James cheating. Even though she doesn't get her own song, Inez plays a key role by showing how sometimes, it's the outside chatter that shakes things up in relationships.

Lyrics That Speak to Me and Why

Music has the unique power to reach deep into our hearts, and Taylor Swift's lyrics have a way of speaking directly to our experiences, emotions, and dreams. Her songs are like diary entries, each one reflecting different facets of life, love, and self-discovery. This page is your canvas to explore the Taylor Swift lyrics that resonate with you on a personal level.

The Lyrics That Feel Like Home

Start by jotting down the Taylor Swift lyrics that feel familiar, like they were written just for you. What memories or feelings do they evoke?

A Line That Changed My Perspective

Is there a particular lyric that shifted the way you see a situation or yourself? Write about the moment of realization and how it impacted you.

Lyrics That Lift Me Up

We all have those go-to songs for when we need a boost. Which Taylor Swift lyrics give you strength or comfort in tough times?

The Soundtrack to My Dreams

What lyrics inspire you to chase after your dreams or remind you of your aspirations? Describe how these words motivate you.

A Verse for My Heartbreak

Taylor Swift is known for her heartbreak anthems. Which lyrics have been a friend to you during a breakup or a tough time in a relationship?

Lyrics That Make Me Dance

Life isn't all about the deep moments. Which Taylor Swift lyrics make you want to get up and dance, carefree and full of joy?

The Lyrics I Wish I Wrote

If you could have penned any Taylor Swift lyric, which one would it be and why? What is it about those words that you connect with so deeply?

Embracing SWIFTIE Culture

Swiftie culture is much more than just being a fan of Taylor Swift's music; it's about being part of a global community that shares love, support, and understanding. This vibrant community celebrates everything.

Taylor stands for, creating traditions and sharing stories that connect Swifties from all corners of the world. From waiting eagerly for Easter eggs in Taylor's videos to crafting handmade bracelets and organizing massive fan projects, Swiftie culture is rich with traditions that make being a fan an experience in itself.

Tailor-Made Outfits

Concerts are not just about the music; they're also about expressing your fandom through creative, often handmade, outfits inspired by Taylor's songs, music videos, or specific lyrics. These costumes create a colorful and welcoming atmosphere at shows, allowing fans to showcase their creativity and celebrate their favorite moments from Taylor's career.

The Easter Egg Hunt

Taylor Swift is famous for hiding Easter eggs in her music, videos, and social media posts, leading fans on thrilling hunts for clues about new music or secret messages. Sharing theories and discoveries has become a beloved tradition, bringing Swifties together in a shared detective work that sparks joy and camaraderie.

"Taygating" Parties

Before concerts, Swifties often gather for "Taygating" parties, where fans meet up to sing Taylor's songs, share stories, and make new friends. These gatherings are a testament to the community's spirit, where the love for Taylor's music creates lasting bonds between fans.

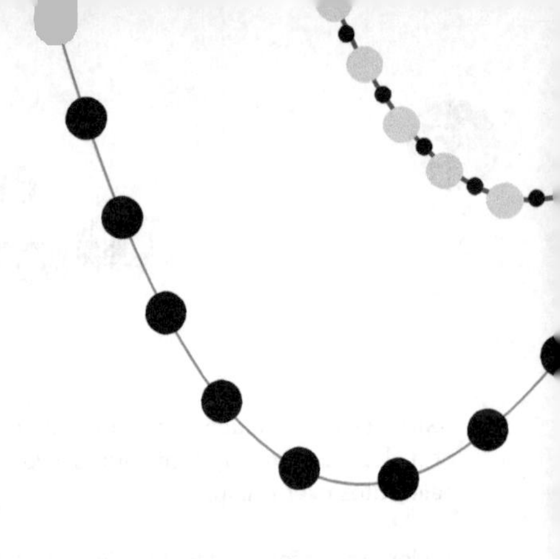

Swiftie Bracelets

Inspired by a lyric from "Midnights," Swifties have embraced the tradition of making and sharing friendship bracelets. This craft has become a symbol of connection within the community, with fans exchanging bracelets at concerts, meetups, and even through mail as a way to show support and friendship.

Fan Projects

Swifties are known for organizing large-scale projects to show their love and appreciation for Taylor, from charity fundraisers in her name to coordinated light shows at concerts. These projects not only celebrate Taylor's impact but also highlight the positive and collaborative spirit of the Swiftie community.

Sharing Personal Stories

Perhaps the most heartwarming aspect of Swiftie culture is the sharing of personal stories about how Taylor's music has touched lives. Whether it's finding comfort in her lyrics during tough times or feeling inspired to pursue one's dreams, Swifties often share these stories online, at concerts, or in fan meetups, creating a space of mutual support and understanding.

Creating the perfect Taylor Swift playlist is an art form. Whether you're gearing up for a long drive, need some tunes for a heartbreak healing session, or are throwing a Swift-themed party, there's a Taylor song for every occasion. Here's how to curate your Taylor Swift playlist to match your mood, event, or even just your day-to-day life.

1 Define the Vibe

Start by deciding what you need this playlist for. Is it upbeat and dancey for a party? Calm and soothing for a chill night in? Or maybe a mix of empowerment anthems for when you need a confidence boost? Taylor's discography can cater to any mood.

2 Mix the Eras

Start by deciding what you need this playlist for. Is it upbeat and dancey for a party? Calm and soothing for a chill night in? Or maybe a mix of empowerment anthems for when you need a confidence boost? Taylor's discography can cater to any mood.

3 Deep Cuts and Hits

While it's easy to lean on Taylor's biggest hits, diving into her albums for those deep cuts can add depth to your playlist. Tracks like "All Too Well" (the 10-minute version for the brave), "Dear John," or "august" showcase Taylor's storytelling prowess and provide a richer listening experience.

4 Theme It Up

Consider creating themed playlists. "Taylor's Love Stories" could feature all her best love songs across eras, while "Swiftie Workout" could pump you up with her most energetic tracks. "Taylor's Tearjerkers" might be just what you need for a good cry.

Tips for the Ultimate Taylor Swift Playlist

Start Strong and End on a High Note

Begin with a song that grabs attention and wrap up with a track that leaves you wanting more. A strong opener could be an upbeat track like "Shake It Off," while a powerful closer might be an anthemic number like "Long Live."

Balance the Tempo

Mixing up fast-paced songs with slower ballads keeps your playlist interesting. After a couple of high-energy tracks, slow things down with a heartfelt ballad before ramping up again.

Don't Forget Live Versions and Covers

Taylor's live performances often give a new life to her songs. Adding a live version of "Wildest Dreams" or her cover of "Can't Stop Loving You" can spice up your playlist with some unexpected flavors.

Use Transitions Wisely

Pay attention to how songs flow into each other. A jarring jump from "Back to December" to "ME!" might disrupt the mood. Consider the end and start of each song to make transitions smooth.

Update Regularly

Taylor's always giving us new material, and your feelings about songs can change over time. Keep your playlist fresh by adding new releases and revisiting old tracks to see if they fit your current vibe.

Taylor's Most Inspirational Quotes

"Life isn't how to survive the storm, it's about how to dance in the rain."

"Never believe anyone who says you don't deserve what you want"

"You need to be happy with yourself or you'll never be able to be happy in a relationship."

"The term trying to forget someone is so awful because you'll never forget someone if you're trying to forget them."

"Don't worry. You may think you'll never get over it. But you also thought it would last forever."

"We don't wish for the easy stuff. We wish for big things. Things that are ambitious, out of reach."

"I've questioned everything about myself, every step of the way. You have to have the same amount of fear and self-doubt as you do hope and blind optimism."

"Fixing your heartbreak by getting into another relationship is not the way to live your life – you need to live it on your terms for a while."

"I'm not concerned with people seeing me in a certain way. Some people see me as a kid, some people see me as an adult. But I'm seriously not going to complain how anybody sees me, as long as they see me."

"Just be yourself, there is no one better.

"If you're lucky enough to be different, never change."

"Fearless is having the courage to say goodbye to someone who only hurts you, even if you can't breathe without them."

"You can stay the same person you've always been even if everything around you changes."

"As soon as I accomplish one goal, I replace it with another one. I try not to get too far ahead of myself. I just say to myself, 'All right, well, I'd like to headline a tour,' and then when I get there, we'll see what my next goal is."

"No one has the right to criticize you for how your body looks, but they will. One thing I've learned from experiencing this exact kind of criticism is that no one else can label your body except for you. No one gets to have a place in your mind if they weren't invited there by you. So please do me this one favor: Don't let their ugly words into your beautiful mind."

"My hope for the future, not just in the music industry, but in every young girl I meet...is that they all realize their worth and ask for it."

"Love always ends differently and it always begins differently – especially with me."

"The longer you're with the wrong person, you could be completely overlooking the chance to meet the right person."

"If you write, you can turn your lessons into your legacy."

49 What Taylor Swift Means to Me

Taylor Swift is more than just a musician to her fans; she's a source of inspiration, a confidant through her lyrics, and for many, a beacon of strength and resilience. Her journey from a young country singer to a global pop icon mirrors the growth and challenges many of us face in our own lives. This page is a space for you to reflect on what Taylor Swift means to you personally. How has her music influenced your life, your choices, and how you see the world?

First Encounters

Recall the first time you heard a Taylor Swift song. What was the song, and what initial impression did it leave on you? How did you feel?

Soundtrack of My Life

Think of moments in your life that a Taylor Swift song has soundtracked. What song comes to mind, and what memory does it hold?

Lyrics That Resonate

Is there a specific Taylor Swift lyric that feels like it was written just for you? Describe the lyric and why it feels personal.

Taylor's Evolution

Taylor's musical journey has seen many changes. How has her evolution as an artist mirrored changes in your own life?

Concert Experiences

If you've ever been to a Taylor Swift concert, describe the experience. How did it feel to be part of that moment, and what memories do you cherish from it?

Empowerment and Inspiration

How has Taylor Swift inspired you or empowered you to take action in your own life? It could be through her music, her actions, or her words.

A Message to Taylor

If you could send a message to Taylor Swift, what would you say? How has her music touched your life?

Taylor's Impact on Fashion and Pop Culture

Taylor Swift is not just a trailblazer in music; her influence on fashion and pop culture is equally remarkable. As she journeyed from a country sensation to a pop and indie icon, her style evolved, setting trends and inspiring fans around the globe. Each era of her music has been accompanied by a distinct fashion statement, making Taylor a true fashion icon!

✦ From Country Charm to Pop Glamour

Starting with cowboy boots and sequined dress Taylor set the stage for country chic, using traditional garments with youthful charm. As sh transitioned into pop, her style evolved into a more sophisticated and glamorous look, embracing crop tops, high-waisted shorts, and sleek evening gowns. This transformation inspi fans to experiment with their own styles, mirro Taylor's growth and versatility—and it shows in the outfits they wear in The Eras Tour!

✦ Shifting Styles

With "Reputation," Taylor introduced a darker, more edgy aesthetic. Leather jackets, thigh-high boots, and even darker lipstick became her new staples, marking a significant shift in her fashion journey. She went back to pastel hues in the "Lover" era, shifted again to grays, browns, and neutrals during "folklore" and "evermore," and went back to retro looks during "Midnights"—a clear proof of how she rocks every fashion style there is!

The Friendship Bracelet Phenomenon

The spike in popularity of friendship bracelets among fans, inspired by lyrics from her song "You're On Your Own, Kid," demonstrates Taylor's influence on not just fashion but also on creating a sense of community and connection among her audience. This trend has seen fans sharing handmade bracelets, embodying the spirit of friendship and unity that Taylor's music promotes.

Bangs Through the Years

Taylor has also made a significant impact with her hairstyles, particularly her bangs, which have become a signature look throughout the years. From her curly country days to her sleek pop era, Taylor has shown that bangs can be versatile and stylish, inspiring fans to adopt similar hairstyles and embrace their own unique look.

Through her evolving style, engagement with fans, and promotion of positive messages, Taylor has cemented her status as a pop culture icon. Her ability to inspire trends, foster a sense of community among her fans, and remain true to her personal style makes her a lasting figure in the fashion world and beyond.

Taylor's Love For Easter Eggs in Music Videos

Taylor Swift, the queen of hidden messages, is known for making her music videos into treasure hunts, leaving Swifties everywhere buzzing with excitement. From the early days of her debut album to the latest releases, Taylor's knack for embedding Easter eggs has become legendary. Here's a look at some of the most beloved hidden gems and what they reveal about the pop icon's creative genius.

A Sweet Surprise in "I Bet You Think About Me"

In the **"I Bet You Think About Me"** music video, fans were treated to a towering wedding cake, each layer dripping with hidden meanings. The top layer boasted the lucky number 13, signaling Taylor's favorite number. Middle layers featured icing depictions of Red (Taylor's Version) rings, a nod to both the past and present eras of the album. The base was adorned with birds, either a wink at the seagulls from her 1989 album cover or a clever play on her surname, Swift. The cake's red velvet interior? A cheeky callback to the **"Blank Space"** video's infamous cake scene.

Name Drops in "...Ready For It?"

Taylor's return with reputation was marked by edginess and intrigue, with **"...Ready For It?"** leading the charge. Fans spotted the name Joseph, a tribute to her then-boyfriend Joe Alwyn, in various forms throughout the video, alongside their birth years, hinting at their deep connection.

Symbolic Accessories in "Out Of The Woods"

"Out Of The Woods," rumored to be about Harry Styles, featured a poignant moment where Taylor discards a necklace off a cliff. This act referenced the end of a relationship, symbolized by the paper plane necklaces they once shared

The Golden Thread in "Willow"

The release of **"willow"** surprised and delighted fans, serving as a continuation of the **"cardigan"** tale. Taylor holding a golden string symbolized the invisible connections of fate, beautifully tying into the lyrics of **"invisible string"** from **"folklore."**

Album and Single Hints in "ME!"

The **"ME!"** video was a departure from the darker tones of reputation. It cleverly hid the name of Taylor's next album, Lover, in the sky and teased the single **"You Need to Calm Down"** through a French argument between Swift and Brendon Urie.

The Ultimate Easter Egg Compilation in "Look What You Made Me Do"

"Look What You Made Me Do" is an Easter egg bonanza, from the **"Nils Sjöberg"** tombstone to the symbolic snakes. Each scene is packed with nods to Taylor's life, battles, and transformations, making it a Swiftie favorite for easter egg deep dives.

A Tribute to Her Grandfather in "Cardigan"

"cardigan" touched hearts with a photo of Taylor's grandfather, Archie D. Swift Jr., linking to the song **"epiphany"** from folklore.

Standing Up to Scooter in "The Man"

"The Man" music video took a stand against Scooter Braun's control over her masters. Taylor, dressed as a man, urinates on a wall marked with her album titles and a **"No Scooters"** sign!

Taylor's Activism and Philanthropy

Taylor Swift's ascent to billionaire status, marked by the monumental success of her Eras Tour and the record-shattering Taylor's Version albums, is a story not just of artistic triumph but of unparalleled generosity. While the world marvels at her earnings, it's her heart for giving that truly defines her legacy.

A Tradition of Generosity

Taylor's journey of philanthropy is as diverse as her discography, touching everything from local libraries to global disaster relief efforts. In 2011, she donated 6,000 books to a library in Pennsylvania, sparking a tradition of supporting education and literacy. Her compassion extends into healthcare, with significant contributions to cancer research and support for families affected by the disease, a cause close to her heart.

Supporting Fellow Artists

In times of need, Swift has stood by her fellow artists, exemplified by her $250,000 donation to Kesha during a legal battle in 2016. This act of solidarity was more than financial support; it was a powerful statement on the importance of artists supporting each other.

Disaster Relief and Social Causes

Taylor's response to disasters is swift and substantial, with donations like $1 million to Louisiana flood relief in 2016 and another $1 million for Tennessee tornado recovery in 2023. Her support extends to social causes as well, including a significant contribution to the Joyful Heart Foundation for survivors of assault following her own courtroom victory.

Songs with Purpose

Beyond monetary donations, Taylor uses her music to make a difference. The release of **"Ronan"** in 2012, a tribute to a young boy lost to cancer, saw all proceeds directed to cancer charities. Similarly, proceeds from her hits like **"Welcome to New York"** and **"Wildest Dreams"** have supported NYC schools and wildlife conservation, respectively, blending her art with advocacy.

A Personal Touch

Perhaps most touching are the instances where Taylor connects personally with fans and communities. From visiting hospital patients to surprising fans at their weddings and even responding to individual crises with financial aid, Taylor's generosity is as personal as it is profound.

Eras of Giving

The Eras Tour not only showcased her musical evolution but also her commitment to leaving a "positive impact" on every city she visited, with donations to food banks along the tour route. Moreover, her generous bonuses to Eras Tour employees underline her appreciation for those who help bring her vision to life.

A Swift Response to Crisis

In times of global crisis, like the coronavirus pandemic, Taylor didn't hesitate to offer direct support to fans struggling financially, embodying the spirit of compassion and community. Her contributions, often accompanied by heartfelt notes, have offered solace and support to many during their darkest times.

Legacy of Love

Taylor Swift's legacy is not just etched in her music but in the countless lives she's touched through her generosity. From major disaster relief efforts to personal acts of kindness, Taylor exemplifies the power of using one's platform for good. For Swifties, these acts of kindness deepen their admiration for Taylor, not just as an artist but as a beacon of hope and generosity in a world in need of both.

Why Taylor Swift Loves the Number

Have you ever noticed how Taylor Swift and the number 13 seem to pop up together a lot? Well, it's not just a coincidence! For Taylor, 13 isn't just any number—it's her lucky charm. Let's take a quick look at why this number is so special in Taylor's world.

Born on the 13th

It all starts with Taylor's birthday: December 13. Being born on the 13th of the month was Taylor's first sign that 13 might be more than just a number for her.

Lucky Number 13

Taylor has shared many times that 13 has been a lucky number for her. She's had a lot of good things happen on the 13th or when the number 13 is involved. Whether it's winning awards, having amazing concerts, or even sitting in the 13th seat or row, Taylor finds luck when 13 is around.

13 Everywhere!

You've probably seen Taylor write the number 13 on her hand during concerts. But that's not all. From her social media posts to hidden messages in her music videos and album notes, the number 13 appears in all sorts of places, almost like a secret code between Taylor and her fans.

A Symbol of Fearlessness

Some people think of 13 as an unlucky number, but not Taylor. She's turned it into a symbol of fearlessness and good fortune. By embracing something that others might avoid, Taylor shows us that it's okay to be different and to find your own lucky charms.

13 in Her Music

Taylor's connection to 13 isn't just about luck; it's also woven into her music. She often includes references to the number in her songs, and fans love finding and talking about these Easter eggs. It's like a fun game that Taylor and her fans play together.

A Shared Sign with Fans

For Swifties, the number 13 has become more than just Taylor's lucky number—it's a symbol of their connection to her. Seeing the number can remind fans of Taylor and the community they're a part of. It's a small way to feel connected to Taylor and other fans around the world.

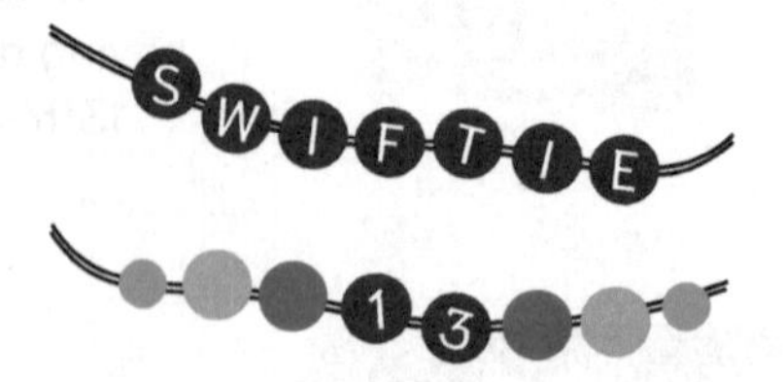

Build a Taylor Swift Concert

Right now, you're not just a fan—you will be the mastermind behind the most epic Taylor Swift concert ever imagined. Let's make a night so unforgettable, it can only exist in the wildest dreams of fans around the globe!

Pick the Venue

- Spectacular Stadium
- Intimate Theater
- Outdoor Festival
- Surprise Location (Your choice!):

Choose the Era: Which Taylor Swift era sets the theme for your show?

- Debut Delights
- Fearless Fantasy
- Speak Now Sparkle
- Red Romance
- 1989 Neon Nights
- Reputation's Edge
- Lover's Dream
- Folklore/Evermore Enchanted Forest
- Midnights Mystique

Dream Setlist: Pick 5 songs that are must-plays at your concert!

Feel free to mix and match across albums!

♫ ____________________

♫ ____________________

♫ ____________________

♫ ____________________

♫ ____________________

Surprise Guest Appearance: Who's joining Taylor on stage for a once-in-a-lifetime duet?

- Another Pop Icon: ________________
- A Legendary Rockstar: ________________
- An Up-and-Coming Artist: ________________
- A Fan from the Audience: ________________

The Encore: What's the one song Taylor closes the show with, leaving everyone breathless?

You've just built the ultimate Taylor Swift concert. Look back at your choices and imagine the magic, the music, and the memories being made. Keep this page as a reminder of the show that would shake the Swiftie universe to its core!

Design the Stage

Now, it's time for you to design Taylor's stage—go crazy and be creative!

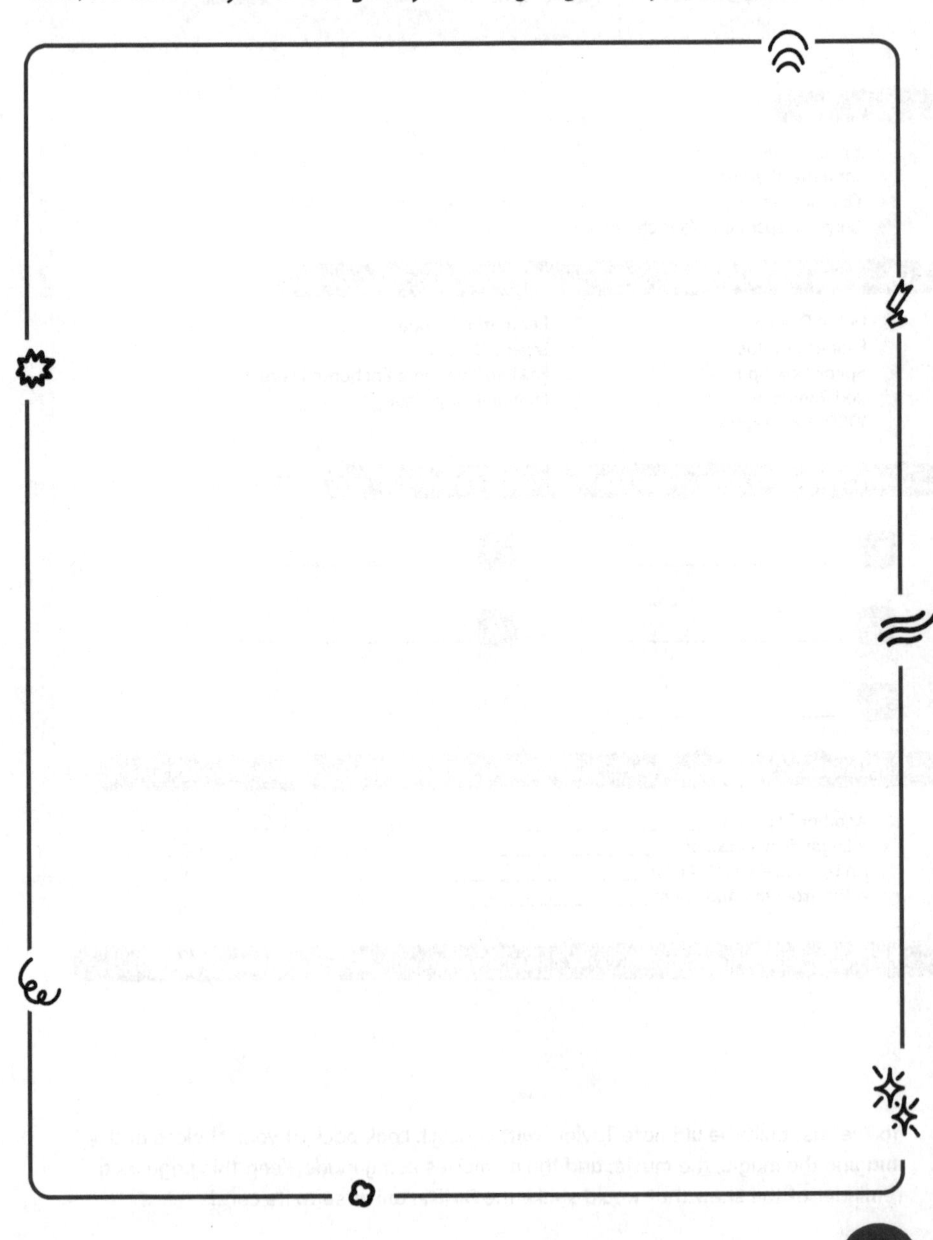

Taylor Swift's Most Iconic Collaborations

"Everything Has Changed" featuring Ed Sheeran (2012)

Taylor Swift's collaboration with Ed Sheeran brought us "Everything Has Changed," a powerful fusion of their storytelling and acoustic power.

"Highway Don't Care" with Tim McGraw and Keith Urban (2013)

Returning to her country roots, Taylor Swift teamed up with country legends Tim McGraw and Keith Urban for "Highway Don't Care."

"Safe & Sound" featuring The Civil Wars (2012)

For "The Hunger Games" soundtrack, Taylor united with The Civil Wars to produce "Safe & Sound," a hauntingly beautiful ballad.

"Bad Blood" featuring Kendrick Lamar (2014)

The remix of "Bad Blood" featuring Kendrick Lamar marked a bold departure for Swift into a pop-rap hybrid, elevated by Lamar's sharp verses.

BONUS

How Well Do Your Friends Know Taylor?

Challenge your friends with our special Taylor Swift quiz, made just for her biggest fans!

Plus, you'll get a free 55-page Taylor Swift activity book that you'll only find in this book!

Scan the QR code or use the link below to see who's the ultimate fan now!

www.swiftiesuperfans.com/ultimate-freebies

Taylor Swift's Most Iconic Collaborations

"I Don't Wanna Live Forever" with Zayn (2017)

Taylor Swift and Zayn Malik's collaboration on "I Don't Wanna Live Forever" became a powerhouse duet filled with intense emotion, making it a standout track among Swift's contributions to films.

"ME!" with Brendon Urie (2019)

Taylor's collaboration with Brendon Urie of Panic! At The Disco on "ME!" delivered a pop anthem rich with self-affirmation and vibrant synth beats, showcasing a fresh bubblegum pop sound that diverged from her usual style.

"Exile" with Bon Iver (2020)

From the album "folklore," "Exile" features Bon Iver and has been lauded for its deep, emotional exploration of a relationship's end. The duet between Taylor Swift's clear vocals and Justin Vernon's haunting voice reeled in a whole new batch of fans worldwide.

"No Body, No Crime" featuring HAIM (2020)

On her "evermore" album, Taylor's "No Body, No Crime" with HAIM tells a gripping story of revenge with a country-rock twist—just another proof of Taylor killing it (ha!) with these fictional stories.

Cook Like Taylor!

Jamie Oliver's Chicken Fajitas

Check out one of Taylor's favorite recipes, inspired by Jamie Oliver's take on Chicken Fajitas! This dish is a burst of color and flavor, perfect for a fun and casual dinner party!

Ingredients You'll Need:

For the Fajitas:

- 1 red bell pepper
- 1 medium red onion
- 2 skinless, free-range chicken breasts
- 1 teaspoon smoked paprika
- A pinch of ground cumin
- 2 limes
- Olive oil
- 4 small or 2 large flour tortillas
- 150 ml fat-free natural yogurt
- 50 g Cheddar cheese

For the Salsa:

- ½ to 1 fresh red chili (to taste)
- 15 ripe cherry tomatoes
- A bunch of fresh coriander (30g)
- 1 lime
- Extra virgin olive oil

For the Guacamole:

- A small handful of mixed-color ripe cherry tomatoes
- ½ to 1 fresh red chili
- A few sprigs of fresh coriander
- 1 ripe avocado
- 1 lime

1 Prep the Stage

- Fire up your griddle pan on high. Slice your red pepper, onion, and chicken into long, thin strips.
- Toss these in a bowl with the smoked paprika and cumin.
- Squeeze over half a lime, add a drizzle of olive oil, season with black pepper, and mix well.
- Let it marinate for a short while as you prep the salsa.

2 Salsa Time

- Finely chop the chili and tomatoes, and roughly chop the coriander (yes, stalks too).
- Mix these in a bowl with a pinch of salt and pepper.
- Squeeze in the juice of 1 lime, and add a splash of extra virgin olive oil.

3 Grill and Thrill

- Place your pepper, onion, and chicken on the griddle.
- Cook for 6-8 minutes until the chicken is golden and the veggies are just charred.
- Keep everything moving to avoid burning.

4 Guac in a Flash

- Squish the cherry tomatoes onto a board, add the chili and coriander, and chop finely.
- Halve the avocado and squeeze out the flesh.
- Chop it all together with lime juice until smooth. Season to taste.

5 Serve It Hot

- Warm your tortillas, then squeeze the remaining lime juice over the sizzling pan.
- Serve the chicken and veggies hot from the pan (be careful, it's hot!).
- Put the yogurt, guacamole, and salsa on the side, with Cheddar cheese ready to grate over the top.

Cook Like Taylor!

Chocolate Chunk Oatmeal Cookies

Here's another recipe that's close to Taylor Swift's heart: Chocolate Chunk Oatmeal Cookies. Let's get started on these delightful treats that are perfect for sharing, gifting, or enjoying with a cup of your favorite beverage!

Ingredients You'll Need:

- 2 cups of all-purpose flour
- 1 cup of rolled oats for that perfect chew
- 1 teaspoon of baking powder for a nice rise
- 1/2 teaspoon of ground cinnamon for a hint of warmth
- 1/2 teaspoon of kosher salt to balance the sweetness
- 1 cup of brown sugar, packed with molasses flavor
- 1/2 cup of granulated sugar for that sweet crunch
- 2 sticks of unsalted butter, room temperature
- 2 large eggs, the binder of our delicious dough
- 1 teaspoon of vanilla extract for that classic cookie taste
- 12 ounces of dark chocolate, roughly chopped into generous chunks
- 1 cup of walnuts, chopped for a nutty bite
- Large flake sea salt for garnish, adding a sophisticated finish

Let's Bake It

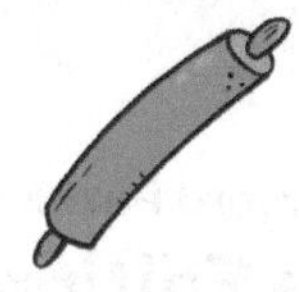

1. **Start by Preheating**
   Turn your oven to 350°F (175°C) and get a baking sheet ready by lining it with parchment paper. This ensures your cookies don't stick and are easy to remove.

2. **Mix the Dry Ingredients**
   In a smaller bowl, whisk together your flour, oats, baking powder, cinnamon, and kosher salt. This combo is the secret to the cookies' texture and flavor.

3. **Cream Butter and Sugars**
   In your stand mixer's bowl, cream together the brown sugar, granulated sugar, and butter until the mixture is light and fluffy. This step is crucial for getting that perfect cookie texture.

4. **Eggs and Vanilla**
   Add the eggs one at a time, making sure each is well incorporated before adding the next. Then, mix in the vanilla extract for that irresistible aroma and flavor.

5. **Combine Dry with Wet**
   Slowly add your dry ingredients to the mixer on a low setting. Stop as soon as everything is just combined to avoid overmixing. Gently fold in your chocolate chunks and walnuts by hand, distributing them evenly throughout the dough.

6. **Scoop and Space**
   Using a spoon, create 2-tablespoon-sized balls of cookie dough. Place them on your prepared baking sheet, leaving about 2 inches between each for them to spread out.

7. **Bake to Perfection**
   Slide your tray into the oven and bake for 12-13 minutes, or until the edges start to turn golden. Watch closely to ensure they don't overbake.

8. **The Finishing Touch**
   As soon as they're out of the oven, sprinkle each cookie with a pinch of sea salt. This not only enhances the flavors but also adds a touch of elegance.

9. **Cool and Enjoy**
   Let the cookies sit on the baking sheet for about 3 minutes to set before moving them to a cooling rack.

Crossword Puzzle: Swiftie Edition

Across

3. A song from 'folklore' that is also a month
5. The city first mentioned in the '1989' album
6. Taylor's middle name
7. Taylor's black-themed album with snake aesthetics
10. The first name of Taylor's cat she met on the set of 'ME!'
11. Best believe I'm still __________
12. The color of Speak Now

Down

1. It's a cruel ______
2. The title of Taylor's documentary on Netflix
4. Taylor's favorite animal
6. The name of Taylor's best friend from high school
8. City where Taylor launched her career
9. Taylor's birthday falls on this month

Across

1. A song that Taylor sings at the end of The Eras Tour
5. Snow on the __________
6. A song from 'evermore' featuring The National
7. A song from 'evermore' in which the intro sounds like banging pots and pans
9. The name of Taylor's grandmother who she wrote a song about
11. 'Nothing good starts in a ____________'

Down

1. A pop singer featured in the 'You Need To Calm Down' music video
2. 'I like shiny things, but I'd marry you with
3. A song on 'Speak Now' featuring Fall Out Boy
4. The previous owner of Taylor's Rhode Island house, mentioned in 'the last great american dynasty'
7. __________ Like Me
8. Taylor's song with the Big Red Machine
10. Taylor is a close friend of the ____ sisters

Let's Play Word Search!

H	I	R	R	Z	R	U	F	W	A	R	S	D
L	T	N	E	O	I	E	J	O	F	E	P	N
T	J	I	S	P	A	B	R	L	W	D	A	I
M	N	R	D	R	U	E	K	G	S	S	R	M
O	Q	M	L	E	V	T	X	R	H	C	K	R
B	H	E	X	O	R	W	A	E	V	A	S	E
D	S	L	L	U	Q	E	K	T	X	R	F	T
S	C	I	N	G	Z	I	M	F	I	F	L	S
L	H	T	N	I	R	Y	B	A	L	O	Y	A
G	O	R	G	E	O	U	S	J	B	N	N	M
D	E	L	I	C	A	T	E	W	E	T	P	C
T	H	G	I	L	Y	A	D	V	Y	B	A	O
Q	F	W	M	I	D	N	I	G	H	T	S	R

AFTERGLOW
DAYLIGHT
DELICATE
FEARLESS
GORGEOUS
LABYRINTH
LOVER

MASTERMIND
MEREDITH
MIDNIGHTS
REDSCARF
REPUTATION
SPARKSFLY

A Twist!

This Word Search Has A Hidden Message In It!

First, locate all the listed words within the puzzle. Fill in these unused letters in the provided blanks to discover the secret message!

E	L	Y	T	S	K	A	Y	R	M	T	A	S	S	W
A	R	E	D	L	A	X	I	N	S	N	E	G	O	T
H	O	U	G	E	H	T	H	U	A	V	Q	N	L	U
Q	K	J	Q	M	R	P	G	O	E	H	D	M	E	X
M	E	T	F	G	S	U	Q	N	Q	E	P	V	O	T
R	B	R	I	O	A	X	Q	E	R	O	I	I	Z	R
B	E	F	O	N	L	H	F	L	Z	L	W	V	P	L
L	E	V	S	M	C	K	A	X	G	I	Y	I	N	E
I	G	J	O	B	R	N	L	N	V	V	O	Y	I	D
H	F	A	E	L	D	E	O	O	R	I	W	X	B	S
V	N	T	U	W	R	L	V	E	R	A	P	W	L	R
F	T	G	T	D	E	I	D	E	S	E	B	A	Y	G
Y	A	H	P	A	K	L	H	C	T	I	L	G	D	K
X	N	J	G	S	U	Y	E	T	G	K	K	J	W	R
O	F	S	O	X	V	H	Z	D	N	F	L	D	Q	D

AUGUST
BEJEWELED
BETTY
EPIPHANY
EVERMORE
FOLKLORE
GLITCH
LONGLIVE
LOVER
OLIVIA
RED
SEVEN
STYLE
WONDERLAND

Write the secret message here:

___ ___ ___ ___ ___'
___ ___ ___ ___ ___
___ ___ ___ ___

___ ___ ___ ___ ___
___ ___!

QUIZ TIME!

Which Taylor Swift Song Character Are You?

Take this quiz to find out which character from Taylor Swift's "folklore" universe best represents you. Answer each question by choosing the option that resonates most with you. Tally your points according to the choices you make to discover which character you are!

When faced with a difficult decision, how do you respond?

A	With a heavy heart, pondering on the what-ifs	2 POINTS
B	By taking a step back to analyze and learn	4 POINTS
C	By letting your emotions guide you	3 POINTS
D	By seeking out truths and uncovering hidden layers	1 POINT

What's your go-to method for dealing with heartbreak?

A	Crafting apologies, hoping for another chance	2 POINTS
B	Seeking solitude to find inner peace and strength	4 POINTS
C	Holding onto memories, struggling to let go	3 POINTS
D	Distancing yourself to gain a clearer perspective	1 POINT

In your circle, what role do you resonate with the most?

A	The healer, mending broken bridges	2 POINTS
B	The philosopher, pondering life's mysteries	4 POINTS
C	The nostalgic, cherishing every memory	3 POINTS
D	The investigator, always digging deeper	1 POINT

Which of these scenarios feels most like a chapter from your life?

A	Seeking forgiveness for past mistakes	2 POINTS
B	Embarking on a journey of self-discovery	4 POINTS
C	Wrestling with the echoes of what once was	3 POINTS
D	Unraveling secrets, learning the truths of your tale	1 POINT

Your ideal evening involves:

A	Crafting letters to reconnect with old friends	2 POINTS
B	Meditating or reading to enrich your soul	4 POINTS
C	Reminiscing about past adventures and loves	3 POINTS
D	Engaging in lively debates about mysteries and anecdotes	1 POINT

Your dream journey would take you to:

A	Places filled with memories, both sweet and bitter	2 POINTS
B	Lands of ancient wisdom and serene landscapes	4 POINTS
C	Hidden corners of the world, rich in romance and mystery	3 POINTS
D	Vibrant cities, where stories unfold at every corner	1 POINT

The soundtrack of your life would be dominated by:

A	Songs of reconciliation and hope for new beginnings	2 POINTS
B	Melodies that speak to personal growth and resilience	4 POINTS
C	Ballads of yearning, filled with bittersweet memories	3 POINTS
D	Dynamic rhythms that challenge perceptions and reveal realities	1 POINT

Which quality in others do you find most admirable?

A	The willingness to repair and rebuild	2 POINTS
B	Deep introspection and the pursuit of truth	4 POINTS
C	Unyielding optimism, despite previous heartbreaks	3 POINTS
D	A straightforward approach, valuing honesty above all else	1 POINT

Results

8–11 Points | **Inez**

You're most like Inez, with a natural talent for unveiling truths. Your insights often shed light on what's hidden, making you an indispensable guide.

12–18 Points | **James**

You embody the spirit of James, whose journey through remorse and redemption illustrates a powerful lesson in forgiveness and the possibility of second chances.

19–25 Points | **Augustine**

Your soul mirrors that of Augustine, marked by deep emotions and a romantic outlook. Despite experiencing loss, your heart remains open to the beauty of what might be.

26–32 Points | **Betty**

Reflecting Betty's resilience, you approach life's ups and downs with wisdom and grace. Your capacity for love and understanding is a beacon for those around you.

My Favorite Taylor Swift Moment

Brainstorm...

Think of a Taylor Swift moment that sparkles brightest in your memory. Whether it's a lyric that felt like a message to your heart, a concert that swept you off your feet, a song that became your personal anthem, or a simple play of her music that shifted your world view—detail that unforgettable time, where you were, what struck you, and why it's engraved in your heart.

Why It's My Favorite

Reflect on why this moment tops your list. Maybe it's the swell of emotions it stirs, how Taylor's lyrics mirrored your life, or the bond it created with her music and fellow fans. Share why this specific Taylor Swift experience holds such a profound place in your life.

Add anything—photos, memorabilia—to visually celebrate this connection. This is your tribute to the moments Taylor Swift's music has crafted just for you!

Write it Down Here!

Date: **Location:**

What I Would Say To Taylor Swift

This section is a dedicated space for you to compose a personal message to Taylor Swift. It's a chance to put into words all the feelings, stories, and gratitude you've harbored towards Taylor and her music. Below are prompts to guide you in crafting your letter. Remember, this is your message; let it reflect your voice and your experiences!

Begin by recounting how Taylor's music first entered your life. What song or album was it? Describe that initial impact and how it drew you in.

Mention the Taylor Swift songs that hold special meaning for you. What are they, and why do they stand out? Share any moments or memories associated with these songs.

Reflect on how Taylor's music has influenced or changed you. Has it offered comfort, motivation, or perhaps a sense of belonging? This is the heart of your message—where you share the depth of your connection to her work.

End with a thank you to Taylor for her music, her resilience, and the inspiration she's provided. Acknowledge the ways in which she's touched your life or the lives of others.

TIP: Feel free to decorate around your letter or add any quotes, lyrics, or drawings that resonate with your message!

Dear Taylor,

Love,

FUN FACTS ABOUT TAYLOR

Taylor wrote her entire "Speak Now" album solo, solidifying her songwriting skills at just 20 years old in October 2010.

She was named after the music legend James Taylor.

After replacing Eric Church on the Rascal Flatts tour in 2006, Taylor gifted Church her first gold record as a thank you.

To reduce the pressures of social media, Taylor turns off comments on her posts, focusing on sharing her life without seeking validation through comments.

Initially planning to name her seventh album "Daylight," Taylor chose "Lover" instead, feeling it better captured the album's essence following "reputation."

Before her rise to fame, Taylor modeled for Abercrombie & Fitch in 2003, joining the ranks of celebrities like Channing Tatum and Jennifer Lawrence who also modeled for the brand.

Growing up on a Christmas tree farm in Pennsylvania, Taylor often reflects on this unique childhood in her music, like in her song "Christmas Tree Farm."

Taylor revealed she has double-jointed elbows in a 2016 Vogue 73 questions video, showcasing it as her unique, if not exactly useful, talent.

Her go-to drink is vodka and Diet Coke, a tidbit she shared in the same Vogue video.

Taylor is the youngest solo artist to win the Grammy for Album of the Year at age 20 for "Fearless" and made history again in 2021 by winning the award three times.

"Lover" sold over 1 million pure copies in the US within a few months of its release.

Taylor's friendships with celebrities like Selena Gomez and her childhood friend Abigail, mentioned in "Fifteen," show her deep connections outside of music.

As the godmother to Jaime King's son Leo Thames, Taylor holds a special place in her friends' families.

Choosing to remove Twitter from her phone, Taylor limits her exposure to overwhelming social media content, focusing instead on political news.

Taylor was named the highest-paid woman in music by Forbes in 2019, earning $185 million that year.

Taylor reserves the fifth spot on her albums for the most emotional ballads, a tradition that fans look forward to with each release.

At the 2019 American Music Awards, Taylor surpassed Michael Jackson to become the most awarded artist in the event's history with 40 wins.

Despite initially dreaming of becoming a stockbroker like her dad, Taylor's true passion for music led her to learn guitar around age 12 and eventually pursue a career in music.

Taylor has expressed that she may never perform "Soon You'll Get Better," a song about her mother's cancer battle, due to it being emotional.

Despite never going to therapy, Taylor considers her mom her confidante, sharing every aspect of her life with her.

The Netflix film "Someone Great" inspired Taylor to write "Death By a Thousand Cuts," demonstrating the impact of storytelling on her songwriting.

Taylor's Legacy: A Look Into Her Influence on Music and Beyond

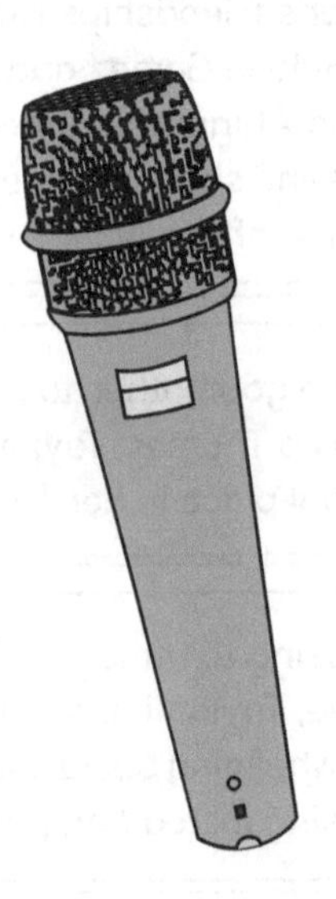

Music Evolution and Songwriting Mastery

Taylor Swift has undeniably transformed the industry of contemporary music, crossing genres from country to pop to indie with unmatched fluidity. Her ability to write relatable, narrative-driven songs has cemented her place as one of the most influential songwriters of our time.

Her fearless approach to sharing personal experiences through her lyrics has not only won her a massive global fan base but also inspired a new generation of songwriters to embrace vulnerability and authenticity in their work.

Breaking Records and Setting New Standards

Throughout her career, Taylor has shattered countless records. From being the youngest solo artist to win a Grammy for Album of the Year to securing the title for the most awarded artist in American Music Awards history, her list of achievements is both long and diverse.

Beyond the trophies and accolades, Taylor has set new standards for what artists can achieve in terms of both creative control and ownership of their music, advocating for the rights of musicians at every level of the industry.

Impact Beyond Music: Advocacy and Philanthropy

Taylor's influence extends far beyond her musical achievements. She's been an outspoken advocate for artists' rights, LGBTQ+ equality, and women's empowerment, using her platform to effect change and encourage her fans to engage with societal issues.

Her philanthropic efforts, from supporting disaster relief efforts to donating to schools and hospitals, reflect a commitment to giving back that is integral to her public persona.

Cultural Influence and Fan Community

The cultural phenomenon of Swifties, Taylor's dedicated fan community, illustrates her impact on music and popular culture. This passionate group not only supports her music but also mobilizes for charitable causes and social justice issues, inspired by Taylor's example.

Taylor's strategic use of social media and direct communication with fans has revolutionized the way artists interact with their audience, setting a new benchmark for fan engagement and community building in the digital age.

Legacy and the Future

Taylor Swift's legacy is marked by her pioneering contributions to music, her unwavering commitment to her artistic vision, and her profound influence on the industry's business practices. As she continues to evolve and challenge expectations, her impact on music and beyond will undoubtedly grow—even bigger than how she is now!

Why We Love Being Swifties: The Magic Between Taylor and Her Fans

Feeling the Music Together

Being a Swiftie means more than just liking Taylor Swift's songs—it's about how her music makes us feel like she's telling our own stories! Taylor shares her ups and downs in her lyrics, making us feel like we're not alone. Plus, she really makes an effort to connect with us, from leaving comments online to surprising fans with gifts, making everything feel even more special.

These actions make us feel like we're part of a big, caring family, where everyone belongs and supports each other, thanks to Taylor's way of bringing us all together.

Standing Up for What's Right

Taylor isn't shy about speaking up for what she believes in, like being kind to everyone no matter who they love or fighting for what's fair. Her bravery inspires Swifties to also stand up for these important issues. This shared belief in making the world a better place brings Swifties even closer together.

It's like we're all part of a team that cares about more than just music—we're united by wanting to help others and make a difference, just like Taylor does.

Connecting Online

The internet is a big place for Swifties—it's where we share our love for Taylor's music, make friends, and even find out clues Taylor drops about her next songs. It's exciting to feel like we're detectives, piecing together hints and sharing our discoveries with friends worldwide.

Why It Feels Good to Be a Swiftie

Being part of the Swiftie community feels amazing because it's about more than music. It's about feeling good about who you are, finding friends who understand you, and being kind to others. Taylor's music brings us together, but it's the friendships and shared moments that keep us here.

Together, we experience the thrill of new music, support each other like a big family, and follow Taylor's lead in spreading kindness and standing up for what's right. It's a unique bond that makes being a Swiftie something really special.

Looking Ahead

As Taylor's music grows and changes, so does the Swiftie community. New songs and albums mean new stories to share, new memories to make, and new reasons to stick together.

Being a Swiftie is about sharing a journey with Taylor and each other. It's a journey filled with music, friendship, and making the world a little better, one song at a time.

13 Life Lessons from Taylor

Aside from full-blown stories, Taylor's works are also infused with so many life lessons embedded within the lyrics. Take a look at some of the most valuable ones...

LESSON 1 **"If you fail to plan, you plan to fail. I laid the groundwork and then, just like clockwork, the dominoes cascaded in a line."**

Building a card tower without a solid base and strategy leads to collapse. Similarly, life requires a blueprint of your goals and the steps to achieve them. This strategy ensures your efforts align with your goals, improving your chances for success!

LESSON 2 **"I'm damned if I do give a damn what people say."**

Worrying about others' opinions is like a boat adrift at sea, pushed around by every passing wind. Instead, take charge of your life's direction. You are the captain, navigating according to your own map. People will always have something to say, but ultimately, your happiness and fulfillment come from living true to yourself, not conforming to others' expectations.

LESSON 3 **"Putting someone first only works when you're in their top five."**

Putting your time and energy to someone who doesn't reciprocate feels as though you're giving away your favorite cake and left without a piece for yourself. It's important to invest in relationships where the appreciation and effort are mutual. Relationships are a balance of give and take, where both parties should value each other's contribution equally.

LESSON 4

"Got swept away in the gray, I just may like to have a conversation."

It's easy to get lost in misunderstandings when we fill in the blanks with our own guesses instead of facts. Sometimes, what we assume about a situation or a person's intentions is way off base, leading us down a path of confusion and sometimes conflict. The remedy? Just talk. Reach out, ask questions, and share your perspective. This open line of communication clears the air, bridges gaps, and often, you'll find that things weren't as complicated as they seemed. Speaking up can turn a potential problem into a simple conversation and strengthen the bond between people.

LESSON 5

"Breathe in, breathe through, breathe deep, breathe out."

In the heat of the moment, our first instinct might be to react immediately. However, taking a step back to breathe and think things through often reveals a better path forward. This moment of pause isn't about hesitation; it's about gaining clarity. By allowing ourselves this space, we can respond rather than react, choosing actions that align with our best selves. A deep breath can be the difference between escalating a problem and resolving it with grace.

LESSON 6

"Got swept away in the gray, I just may like to have a conversation.

It's easy to get lost in misunderstandings when we fill in the blanks with our own guesses instead of facts. Sometimes, what we assume about a situation or a person's intentions is way off base, leading us down a path of confusion and sometimes conflict. The remedy? Just talk. Reach out, ask questions, and share your perspective. This open line of communication clears the air, bridges gaps, and often, you'll find that things weren't as complicated as they seemed. Speaking up can turn a potential problem into a simple conversation and strengthen the bond between people.

LESSON 7 **"Breathe in, breathe through, breathe deep, breathe out."**

In the heat of the moment, our first instinct might be to react immediately. However, taking a step back to breathe and think things through often reveals a better path forward. This moment of pause isn't about hesitation; it's about gaining clarity. By allowing ourselves this space, we can respond rather than react, choosing actions that align with our best selves. A deep breath can be the difference between escalating a problem and resolving it with grace.

LESSON 8 **"You're talking **** for the hell of it. Addicted to betrayal, but you're relevant."**

Gossip can be tempting; it's a quick and easy way to feel connected to others or more important in the social circle. But this false sense of belonging comes at a high cost—trust. Spreading rumors or revealing secrets damages relationships, sometimes beyond repair. True connections are built on a foundation of trust and mutual respect, where private conversations stay private, and personal stories are shared, not stolen. Instead of seeking significance through gossip, aim for genuine interactions that respect everyone's privacy.

LESSON 9 **"Levitate above all the messes made."**

Life's like walking through a field full of pitfalls; drama and chaos can pop up when you least expect it. The trick is learning how to glide over these traps without getting caught in the mess. Staying focused on what's important—your goals, your peace of mind—helps keep you moving forward. Empathy plays a big role too; understanding where others are coming from can prevent a lot of unnecessary conflict. By keeping your eyes on the prize and your heart open to understanding, you can go through life's storms without getting drenched.

LESSON 10 **"Ladies always rise above. Ladies know what people want. Someone sweet and kind and fun. The lady simply had enough."**

In the heat of the moment, our first instinct might be to react immediately. However, taking a step back to breathe and think things through often reveals a better path forward. This moment of pause isn't about hesitation; it's about gaining clarity. By allowing ourselves this space, we can respond rather than react, choosing actions that align with our best selves. A deep breath can be the difference between escalating a problem and resolving it with grace.

LESSON 11

"I have this thing where I get older but just never wiser."

Simply letting the years roll by without pausing to reflect is like sitting on a train watching the scenery blur past. You're moving, but are you really going anywhere? Growing wiser isn't about tallying up birthdays; it's about soaking up lessons from each experience, good or bad. If you glide through life without ever asking, "What can I learn from this?", you're likely to find yourself stuck in the same old patterns. Active learning and self-reflection are the keys to breaking the cycle. Open yourself up to new ideas, challenge your preconceptions, and be willing to change. That's how true growth happens—it's an ongoing process, not a milestone.

LESSON 12

"My smile is like I won a contest. And to hide that would be so dishonest."

Letting people know they've made you happy is a gift, not just to yourself but to them as well. It's like sunshine breaking through clouds; sharing your joy can brighten someone's day in ways you might not even realize. Being open about what makes you happy creates a ripple effect, spreading warmth and positivity. It also deepens your connections with others, making your relationships richer and more meaningful. When you're not afraid to show your happiness or share your gratitude, you open the door to more authentic, heartfelt interactions. It's a way of saying, "You matter to me," and that's something everyone needs to hear.

LESSON 13

"There were pages turned with the bridges burned. Everything you lose is a step you take."

Think of life as a book you're writing. Some chapters might end with a plot twist you didn't see coming, like a bridge burning down behind you. But here's the thing: every time you turn the page on a setback or wave goodbye to something that didn't work out, you're actually stepping forward. Sure, it might not feel like it right away. It's like stumbling in the dark until you find the light switch. But those stumbles? They're teaching you where not to walk next time. Each loss or failure is like a lesson dressed up as a tough day. They're the universe's way of nudging you to look at things differently, to shake up the status quo, and to grow stronger and smarter. So, instead of viewing setbacks as stop signs, see them as signposts, pointing you in a new direction, one that's filled with possibilities and new beginnings. Every step taken, even the ones that felt like falls, is a step toward becoming the person you're meant to be.

Kickstart Your Songwriting Journey—Just Like Taylor!

Ready to dive into songwriting but not sure where to start? Let's get those creative juices flowing! Inspired by Taylor Swift's incredible journey, these prompts are meant to light a spark under your songwriting skills.

Grab your pen, skim through these prompts, and use the next few pages to jot down your thoughts, play with lyrics, and maybe even discover the next big hit.

Prompt 1: The Moment That Made Me
Think of a time that really changed you. What happened, who was there, and how did it make you feel? Write a song that tells the story of that moment, like it's the opening scene of a movie about your life.

Prompt 2: The One That Got Away
Ever had something you wished you said but didn't? Picture that person and what you'd say if you could. Write a song that says all those unsaid things, pouring out your heart in every line.

Prompt 3: Backwards Day
Imagine telling the story of a significant day, but start from the end and go backwards. What made the day stand out, and how would it look if it played in reverse?

Prompt 4: Crossroads
Write about a choice you made that took you on an unexpected adventure. Focus on why you made that choice, the bumps you hit along the way, and where you ended up because of it.

Prompt 5: Love Letter to a Place
Pick a place that means the world to you. It could be where you grew up, a cozy corner in a coffee shop, or even a fantasy world. Craft a song that brings this place to life, sharing why it's so special.

Prompt 6: Rising Above
Think back on a tough challenge you faced and how you beat it. Your song should capture the struggle, the moment things started to turn around, and how you came out stronger on the other side.

Prompt 7: Finding Magic in the Mundane
Ever find yourself inspired by the simplest things? Choose an everyday moment that unexpectedly struck a chord with you. Write a song that finds the magic in that mundane moment.

Prompt 8: Dreaming Big
Picture where you want to be a few years from now. What do you hope to achieve? Write a song to your future self, filled with your dreams, the advice you'd give, and the experiences you hope to encounter.

These prompts are just the beginning. There's a whole world inside you waiting to be turned into music. The key? Just be real, be you, and let your personal stories and dreams shine through your songs. Let's start writing!

Your Creative Space

Now that you've written your first song, it's time to take things to a whole new level! How about making some cover art for your future album? Show us what you've got!

Put your album title here!

BIG BONUS

Claim Your Free 55-Page Taylor Swift Activity Book!

We adore Taylor and her fans just as much as you do!

That's why we're offering a unique 55-page bonus activity book exclusively just for you.

You won't find this book anywhere else! Don't miss out.

Scan the QR code or click the link below to download your special gift now!

www.swiftiesuperfans.com/ultimate-freebies

Made in United States
Troutdale, OR
12/21/2024